The A to Z Book of Wild Animals

To Kath Scott—P.D.S.

Silver Dolphin

Silver Dolphin Books
An imprint of the Baker & Taylor Publishing Group
10350 Barnes Canyon Road, San Diego, CA 92121
www.silverdolphinbooks.com

This edition first published in 2012

ISBN-13: 978-1-60710-592-3
ISBN-10: 1-60710-592-6

Library of Congress Cataloging-in-Publication data available upon request.

Designed by Leonard Le Rolland
Written by Rachel Williams
Edited by Libby Hamilton

Printed in China

1 2 3 4 5 16 15 14 13 12

The A to Z Book of Wild Animals

AN ALPHABET ADVENTURE

Illustrated by
Peter David Scott

Silver Dolphin

San Diego, California

Aa

is for ant. . .

. . .and anteater

Bb
is for butterfly

C c

is for crocodile

D d

is for dolphin

E e
is for
elephant

F f

is for flamingo

G g

is for giraffe

H h

is for hummingbird

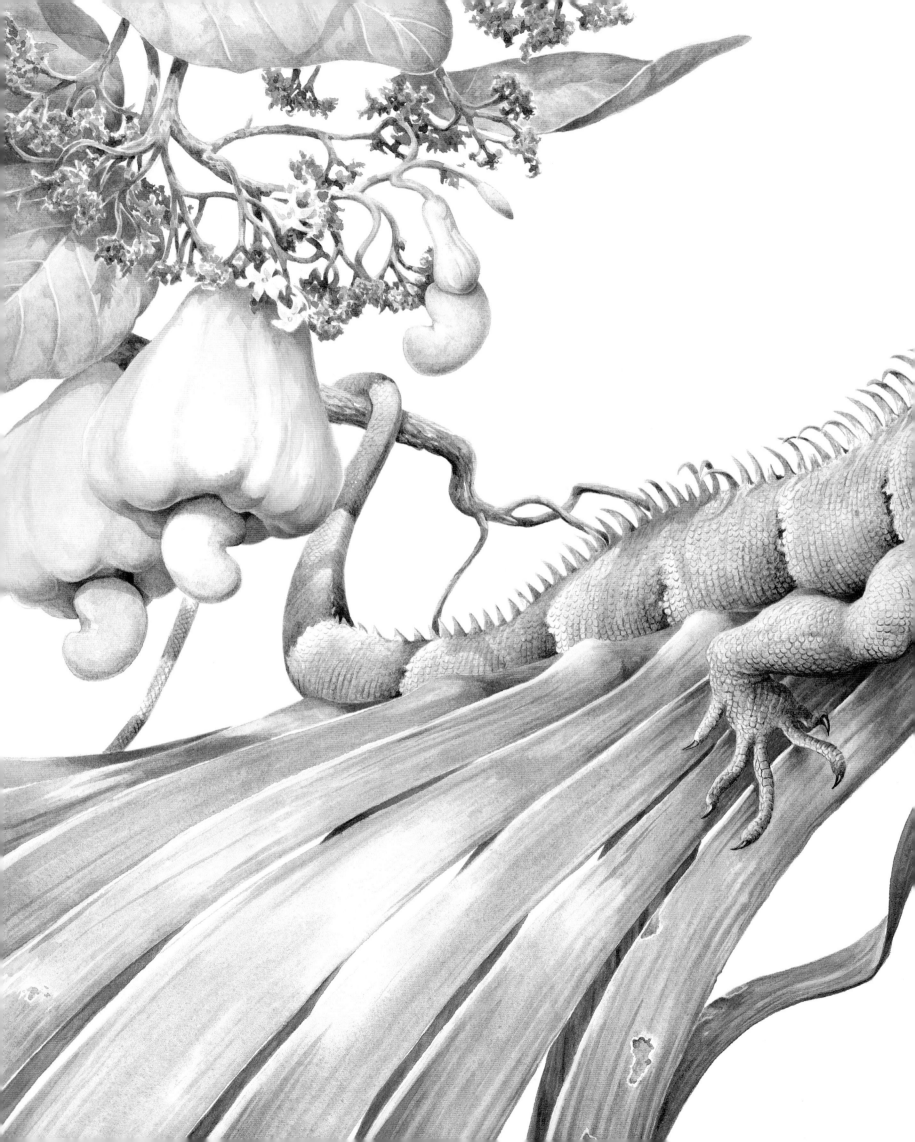

I i
is for iguana

J j

is for jellyfish

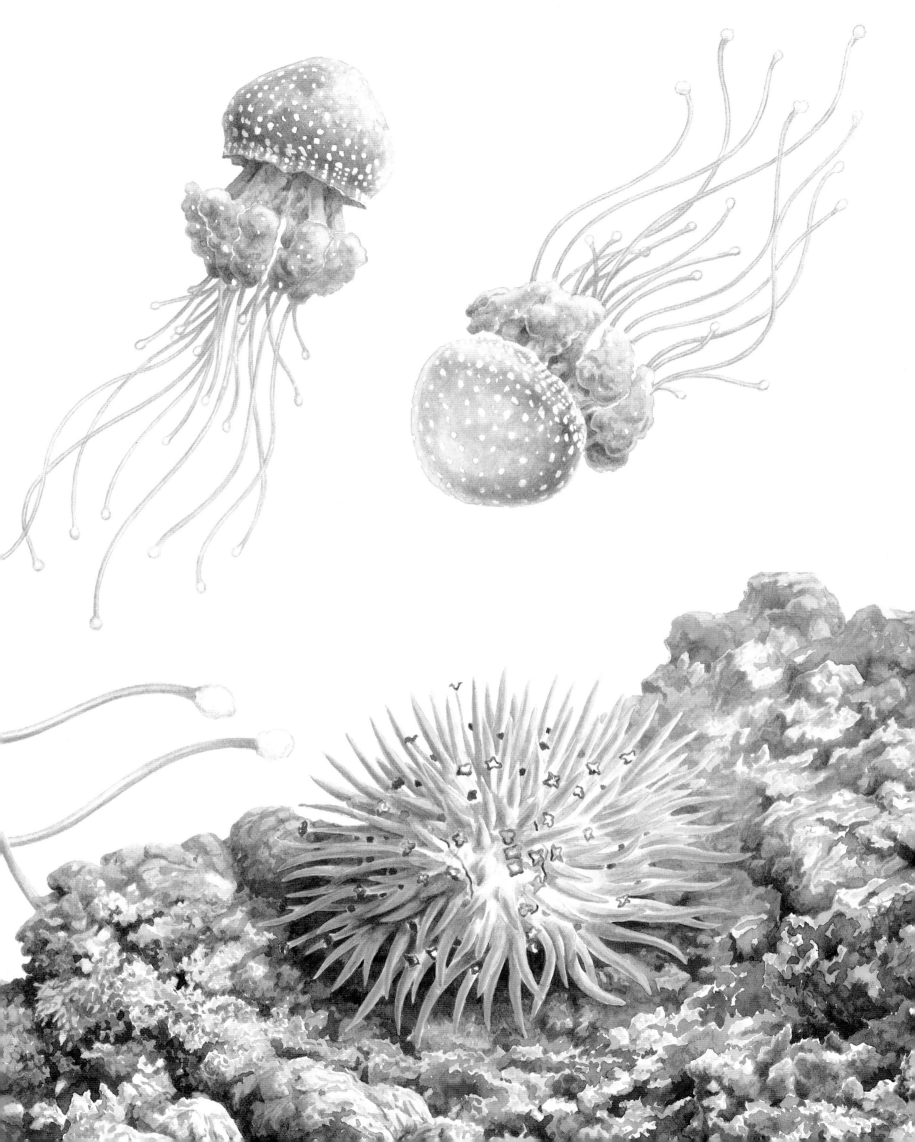

K k

is for
kangaroo

L l
is for leopard

Mm

is for monkey

Nn

is for newt

O o

is for octopus

P p
is for
polar bear

Qq

is for quail

R r

is for rhino

S s

is for shark

T t
is for tiger

U u

is for umbrellabird

V v

is for vulture

W w

is for whale

Xx

is for extinct

Y y
is for yak

Z z

is for zebra

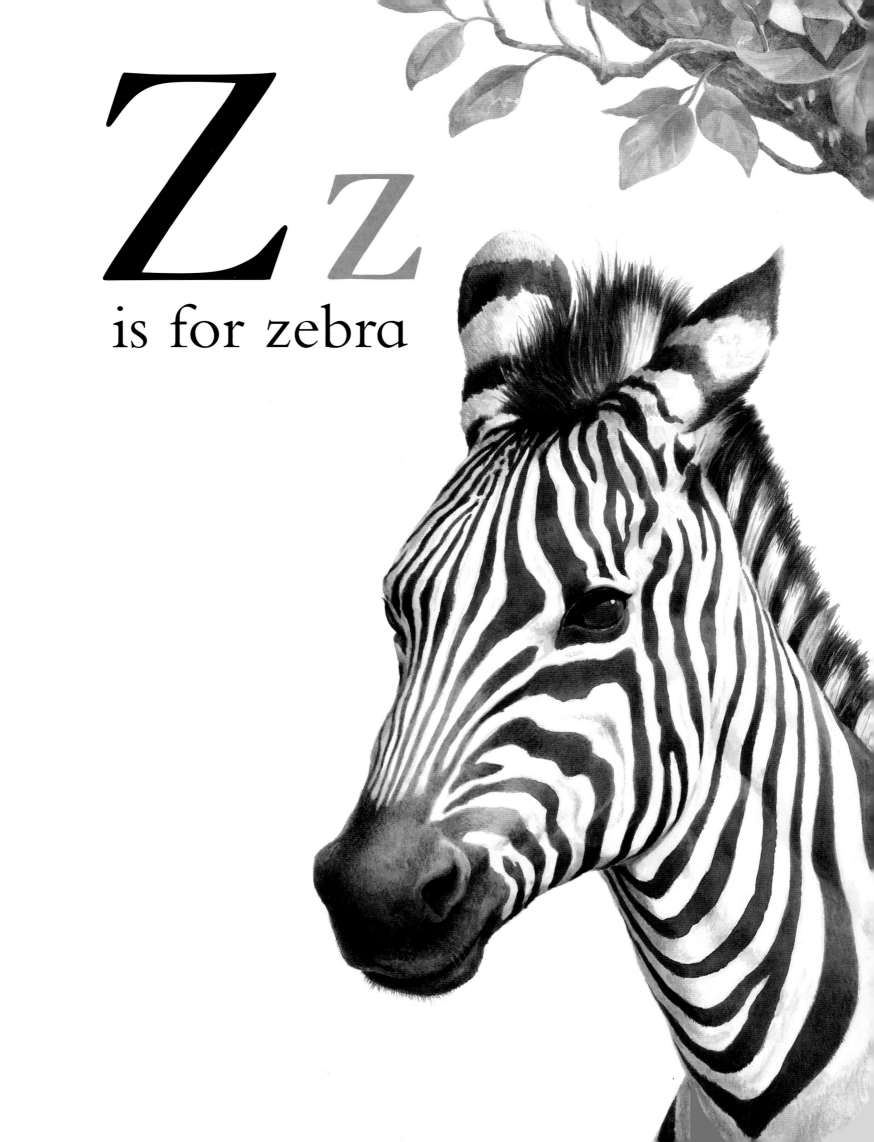

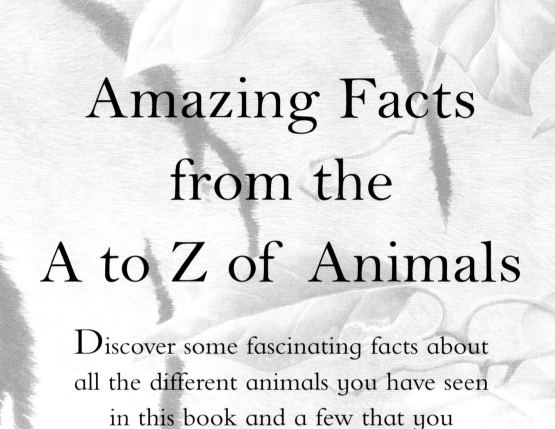

Amazing Facts
from the
A to Z of Animals

Discover some fascinating facts about
all the different animals you have seen
in this book and a few that you
might not have spotted. . .

Leaf-cutter **A**nt

As the line of large worker ants transport leaf pieces, their chief runs up and down the line keeping order while tiny workers ride on top of the pieces to keep flies away. With spindly legs and strong backs, leaf-cutter ants play an important role in the ant colony. The leaf pieces are combined with ant manure, making a compost that feeds the fungus the ants live on and nourishes the wider rain forest.

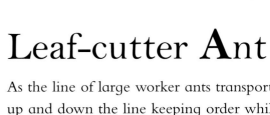

Anteater

Who has a long, sticky tongue covered with hundreds of sharp spines? The anteater, no less! These toothless mammals walk on their knuckles but use their razor-sharp claws and their long, tubelike mouths to open the nests of termites and lick up wandering insects. A giant anteater can stick out its 23-inch tongue twice every second, consuming tens of thousands of ants a day. At night, the anteater will stay warm by covering itself with its long, bushy tail.

Australian Birdwing **B**utterflies

As he fans his wings wide and lifts his antennae high, the male birdwing has every reason to feel proud. Not only is he the largest butterfly species in Australia, but his shimmering green wings, splashed with black and bright yellow, are the sign of a clean environment. Unlike other species of butterflies that can survive anywhere, the Australian birdwing is a rare, precious species that cannot live without a clean home and food that's free from pollution.

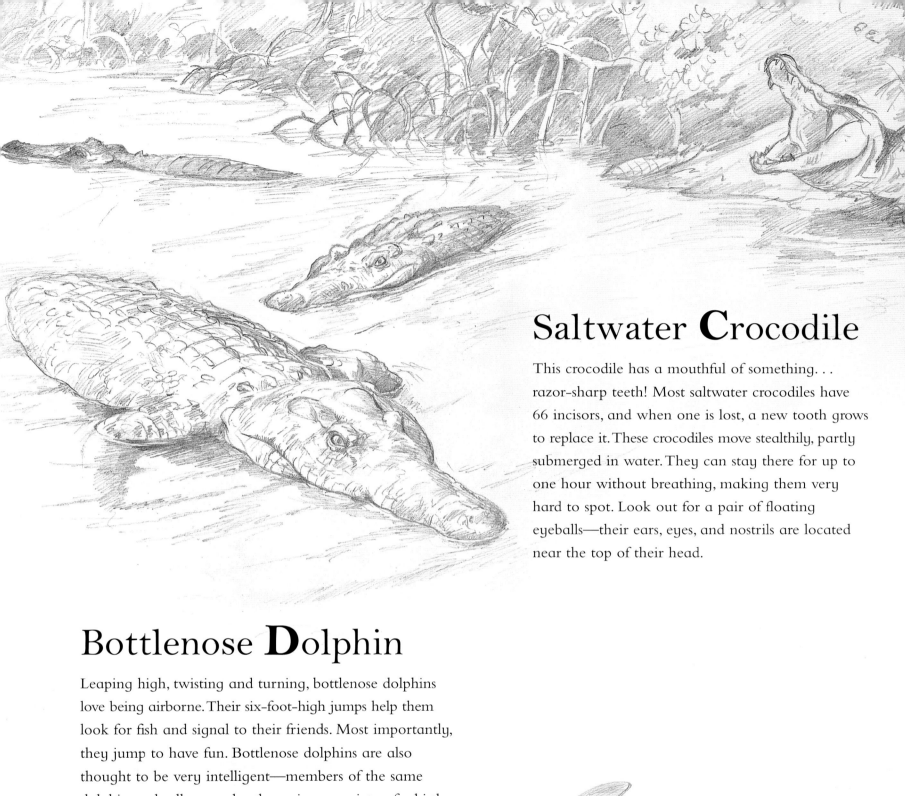

Saltwater **C**rocodile

This crocodile has a mouthful of something. . . razor-sharp teeth! Most saltwater crocodiles have 66 incisors, and when one is lost, a new tooth grows to replace it. These crocodiles move stealthily, partly submerged in water. They can stay there for up to one hour without breathing, making them very hard to spot. Look out for a pair of floating eyeballs—their ears, eyes, and nostrils are located near the top of their head.

Bottlenose **D**olphin

Leaping high, twisting and turning, bottlenose dolphins love being airborne. Their six-foot-high jumps help them look for fish and signal to their friends. Most importantly, they jump to have fun. Bottlenose dolphins are also thought to be very intelligent—members of the same dolphin pod talk to each other using a variety of whistles to say different things. In some fishing villages, bottlenose dolphins cooperate with the local fishermen, driving fish into their nets and eating any that are left over.

Dogfish

It may not be the most menacing of sharks, but the spiny dogfish can take good care of itself. These sharks have two spines, which they use to defend themselves in the murky ocean waters. If captured, the dogfish can arch its back to pierce captors with a protruding fin. The glands at the base of its spines also secrete a mild poison.

Elephant

Like enormous, breezy fans swaying to and fro, the elephant's ears keep the animal cool beneath the burning sun. Elephants are majestic creatures and their long, graceful trunks are unique. They use their trunks like a fifth limb to pluck grass, pull branches, and lift logs. These handy limbs are also used for drinking—and squirting—when water is near.

Egret

The egret is possibly the most handsome bird in the heron family. During the breeding season, it develops fine, milky-white plumes that fall elegantly down its back. In the late 19th century, the species was endangered by fierce hunting, as hatmakers around the world used these plumes for decoration. Normally a nighttime hunter, the hardworking egret will hunt day and night when it has chicks to feed.

Flamingo

It's hard enough trying to stand on one leg—imagine trying to sleep on one! This is just one of the flamingo's amazing abilities: their long legs also help them to wade through thick grasses. The flamingo's beak curls downward, allowing it to filter tiny plants and crustaceans from the water. The foods they eat give the birds their beautiful pink color—they contain carotenoids, the same pigment that makes carrots orange.

Giraffe

If any animal knows what it is like to have its head stuck in the clouds, it's the giraffe. With a long, elegant neck and strong, spindly legs, the giraffe is the tallest living animal on earth. Its height helps the giraffe to eat leaves and fruit from the tall trees that other creatures cannot reach—assisted by its 18-inch-long bluish-black tongue. Despite their height, giraffes are swift runners, and can reach speeds of 21 miles an hour when danger threatens.

Bee Hummingbird

With its bright, brilliant feathers, the bee hummingbird looks like a tiny flying jewel. This magnificent creature is the smallest bird in the world—about the size of a bumblebee. Bee hummingbirds beat their wings up to 80 times a second, and hover like little helicopters above plants, sucking up nectar with their strawlike tongues.

Hairstreak Butterfly

This stunning butterfly gets its name from the unusual hairlike tail it has on each wing. Eye-catching and delicate, the hairstreak, like the hummingbird, prefers to feed on sweet tree sap and nectar.

Iguana

Peer into the thick green jungle and if you're lucky you'll spot a small, prehistoric-looking beast—the iguana. When the male of this reptilian species needs to protect his own space in the jungle, he will drop down his dewlap— a dangling piece of skin—to frighten onlookers. He will also use his tail as a whip against attackers.

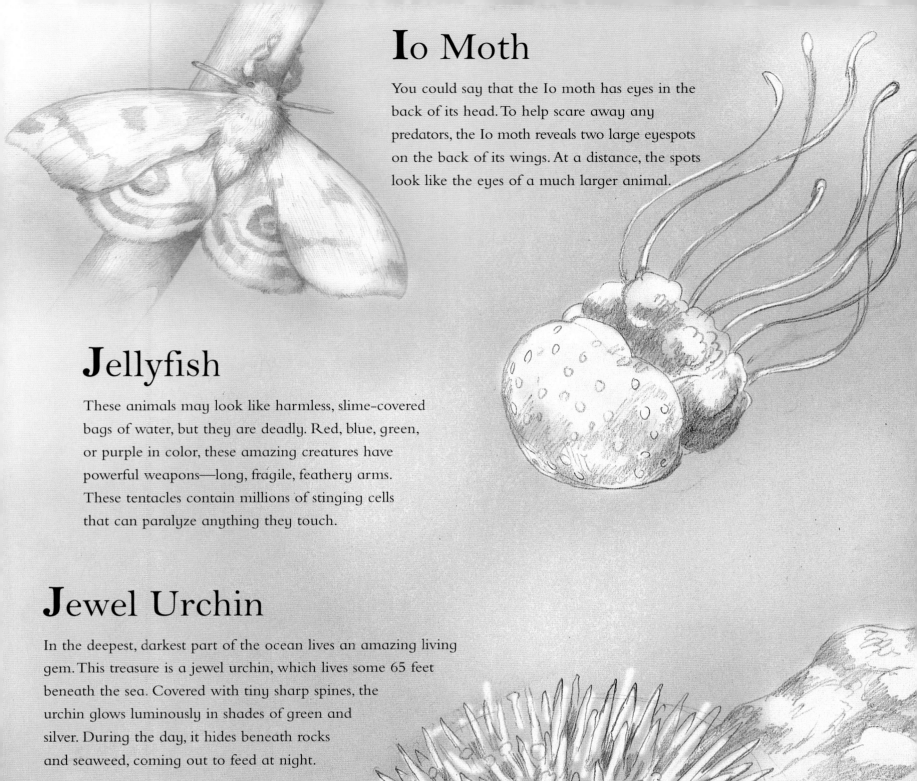

Io Moth

You could say that the Io moth has eyes in the back of its head. To help scare away any predators, the Io moth reveals two large eyespots on the back of its wings. At a distance, the spots look like the eyes of a much larger animal.

Jellyfish

These animals may look like harmless, slime-covered bags of water, but they are deadly. Red, blue, green, or purple in color, these amazing creatures have powerful weapons—long, fragile, feathery arms. These tentacles contain millions of stinging cells that can paralyze anything they touch.

Jewel Urchin

In the deepest, darkest part of the ocean lives an amazing living gem. This treasure is a jewel urchin, which lives some 65 feet beneath the sea. Covered with tiny sharp spines, the urchin glows luminously in shades of green and silver. During the day, it hides beneath rocks and seaweed, coming out to feed at night.

Koala

Koalas may seem like the most huggable creatures on earth, but watch out—they can be grizzly and nasty. They aren't bears, as many people believe, but are more closely related to the kangaroo and wombat family of mammals, carrying their young in a pouch, as the kangaroo does. Chewing on eucalyptus leaves in the shade of a gum tree, the koala will sleep for around 19 hours a day, its thick fur keeping it warm at night and cool on hot days.

Kangaroo

Hippedy-hoppedy-hop, the 'roo hops nonstop! The kangaroo, or "roo" to locals, is a native Australian animal that can leap up to 30 feet in one big jump. These hopping, leaping mammals have long ears that swivel and pick up sounds from any direction. Babies will spend the first 15 months of their lives in their mother's pouch, with a front-row seat in a very bouncy adventure.

Leopard

Awake and hungry, the stealthy leopard will go out to hunt at night. Their night vision is six times better than a human's, and when stalking its prey, it will move silently, its big, padded paws softening its steps. Leopards are solitary animals, living on their own and hunting as individuals. During the day, the leopard will rest in the trees, where the pattern on its coat keeps it hidden.

Blue-and-yellow Macaw

"Skreetch!" exclaims the macaw, greeting his family scattered around the rain forest. These birds are a large species of parrot, their yellows and blues filling the trees with color. Like all creatures on earth, each macaw is different—the pattern of its facial feathers is as unique as a human fingerprint. You might also see the scarlet macaw or the military macaw, which is a striking green color.

Spider Monkey

Swinging from branch to branch, spider monkeys are wonderful tree climbers. Their grasping hands and feet and long, gangly legs help them move quickly between treetops. When their limbs get tired, spider monkeys can swing by their tails, which have skin grooves and grips, making them like strong fingers. These monkeys are intelligent and highly social creatures. Grooming each other with their long, pink tongues is just one of many ways in which they show each other affection.

Nerite Snail

These water snails have gills and can live in both salt water and freshwater. They eat algae, so are often bought for aquariums to keep them tidy. Rarely growing larger than half an inch, these little snails are also cooked and eaten in Southeast Asia!

Great Crested Newt

Great crested newts live on land but breed in water. At night, they hunt insects, worms, and slugs, then rest under shady rocks and logs during the day. Newts are seasonal creatures—in the winter they hibernate on land or in the mud at the bottom of their breeding ponds. During breeding season, you can spot males by the crests that develop on their backs and tails. Newts are also careful parents—each egg is laid individually on a leaf that is then folded over to hide the egg from predators.

Common Octopus

In just one second, the common octopus can change color and skin texture, stopping deep-sea bullies in their tracks. Their eight long tentacles come with two powerful rows of suckers, helping them to grip rocks and prey. The octopus uses jet propulsion by expelling a stream of water to move quickly, and its large eyes enable it to see in the murky ocean waters.

Common Oyster

Among the shallow waters of coastal areas live thousands of little mollusks known as oysters, their soft bodies enclosed in two hinged shells. When sand, grit, or food from the sea gets trapped in between these hinges, the oyster covers the foreign body with a shiny iridescent substance called "nacre" to reduce the irritation. Every day it coats the grit with more nacre, and a pearl is slowly formed. The size of the pearl depends on the size of the original piece of grit.

Polar Bear

The big, white polar bear has one of the best winter coats of all the Arctic creatures. This bear keeps warm with two layers of fur and a layer of fat under its skin, and when walking, uses spongy pads to keep its toes cozy. When in the water, the polar bear's powerful front legs act like paddles, and its back legs help it to steer.

Ptarmigan

You might have missed this unusual bird, because the ptarmigan is seasonally camouflaged—in the snowy winter months its brown feathers molt and are replaced with white ones. The ptarmigan is also a surprisingly friendly bird, because it lives in the Arctic and so is not used to being hunted.

Quail

Within just a few hours of birth, the young quail is able to run and hunt. This baby might grow to be a large, elegant male, or what is generally considered to be a more plain-looking female. Many other birds need fine, colorful plumage, but the female quail's plainness is an advantage—it acts as camouflage, which is particularly useful when sitting on the eggs it lays on the ground.

Rhino

With a sharp, powerful horn and strong back, the rhino is the third-heaviest living animal on earth, with skin that is an inch thick. What this creature lacks in eyesight and agility, it makes up for in speed—a rhino is capable of running up to 28 miles per hour. Made of compressed hair, the rhino's horn is a strong weapon, capable of killing a human.

Great White Shark

Only one predator has earned the nickname "White Death." The great white shark has some of the best weapons of any predator—a torpedo-shaped body to help it move quickly, a sense of smell that can detect blood half a mile away, eyes to see more than 23 feet ahead, and teeth sharp enough to slice through bone. Look out—these creatures were born to be feared!

Tiger

What is the deadliest part of a tiger? Perhaps its 3-inch canine teeth, the largest of all the big cats, or its 5-inch claws? For creatures hunted by this fearsome animal, it is more likely to be its highly developed sense of hearing. With ears that are five times more sensitive than a human's, a tiger can sense the position of its prey from the smallest movement and even determine what kind of animal it is.

Umbrellabird

The umbrellabird is one of the most cunningly clever hunters. Named for its unique fishing technique, this black heron stands in the water, flicks open its wings, and folds them in front of its body. Just like an umbrella, the bird creates a shady area in the water so that prey can be seen more easily. Unsuspecting fish are drawn to this area of shade, thinking it offers protection. But they had better beware!

White-backed Vulture

Soaring over the savanna, the white-backed vulture spots the carcass of an impala and swoops in for dinner. Like other vultures, this creature is a scavenger—happy to feast on leftovers and discarded pieces of meat. Following a feed, it will often wipe itself clean using its white neck ruff—a contrast to its otherwise dark plumage. Its head is bald, because it is the only place that the vulture cannot reach to clean.

Walrus

Also known as the "tooth-walking sea cow," the walrus uses its tusks to haul itself out of the freezing waters onto pack ice. The length of the male's tusks will determine his place in the walrus family, and his success with females. During breeding season, males duck and dive, showing off to the lounging herds of females.

Bowhead Whale

The bowhead whale powers forward, its mouth open wide, tongue flailing. Dining on small animals that float into its open mouth, this peaceful, gentle creature is highly vocal and uses underwater sounds to communicate while traveling, feeding, and socializing. When it needs to breathe while in the frozen Arctic waters, the bowhead breaks the ice from beneath with its massive, bony skull.

Extinct Woolly Mammoth

What happens when one whole family of animals dies out? The species becomes extinct—meaning that it no longer exists anywhere on earth. Long ago, mass extinction of the dinosaurs occurred very quickly, and today, the rate of species extinction is very high. With their long, thick hair and curled tusks, the elephant-like woolly mammoth was the last of its species of mammoth to survive extinction, living until the end of the Ice Age.

Yak

This yak is hungry and, using his 3-foot-long horn to dig in the snow, he searches for food. Well-equipped for the harsh winter weather, this creature has two coats—an outer waterproof layer and a dense, warm undercoat to keep in precious body heat during the coldest months. Many people in Southeast Asia treat the yak as a valuable asset, using it for milk, meat, wool, and transport.

Zebra

For the wandering lion, blind to a variety of colors and confused by patterns, the zebra's stripes make it almost impossible to spot. Like our fingerprints, the pattern on each fantastic coat is unique to every zebra. The zebra lives in herds, and its strong back legs deliver a powerful kick, offering some protection against attack.

Zorilla

Could this be the smelliest animal on earth? The zorilla, a skunklike mammal that lives in Africa, has gland secretions that can be smelled from half a mile away. When alarmed, the zorilla will first raise the hair on its back and lift its tail, making itself look larger. If this does not deter the predator, the zorilla will then use scent glands to spray a strong-smelling fluid at its attacker. Hold your nose!